The Destiny Number 9

Who love cash the most? Men or ladies?

GLEN WATERS

Table of contents

Without a doubt cash is the base, everything being equal, somewhat... This is a story that includes the esteem of cash over adoration.

Chapter 1

"I least anticipated this from you. At any rate, it has previously worked out and I say thanks to God Faustina came to save me. Allow me to see the rundown." He extended forward his hands and I gave them to him. He took the rundown and concentrated on it well overall and grinned. "Haha my person, am certain this rundown is recommending that the woman turns into your property in the wake of wedding her. For what reason would it be a good idea for you to pay your parents-in-law toward the month's end and fuel their vehicle for them? Ok, this is rubbish. It has no importance.

Eemm this is how we will respond, you don't have to camouflage yourself as though you have turned rich. Since the women's mother is prepared to acknowledge you, I will assist you with getting a portion of the things and let them know that was all you had the option to get. Allow them to comprehend that you can't bear paying for their fuel consistently and pay them also. Why, are you a bank where their little girl turns into their store?" He said and tapped my shoulders.

I said thanks to him for the help and exhortation. He said I shouldn't stress. He enlivened me with these words "We as a whole realize that life isn't that straightforward and that all through our excursion in life we could confront various difficulties, issues, and misfortunes. The contrast between individuals who prevail throughout everyday life and the people who don't is their capacity to confront life's difficulties accurately and not the shortfall of difficulties. Agbanavor, I see you be a major area of strength for a strong individual. Furthermore, as such an individual, you will get hit by misfortunes and life's concerns very much like every other person.

On the off chance that I ought to let you know how my dad began before getting where he is currently, you will simply open your mouth wide. As far as I might be concerned, I will say my dad accommodated me so I won't say I went through the thing you are going through now however my dad did. Simply figure out how to confront life's difficulties and that will assist you with climbing to the next level and carry on with a more joyful life." I said thanks to him for such strong words.

He said I ought to do the game plans quickly since he wants to travel abroad in three weeks. He gave me the cash to purchase the most squeezing things on the rundown. I went to illuminate Gift and her family that I was prepared to do the wedding function. Every one of these whiles, the child was not named however Gift continued to call out to him after me Olorunsogo. I went with a portion of the folks chipping away at my managers working to fix the date for the function. You will have a hard time believing it, Gift's dad said he neglected to add harming charge to the rundown. My companions giggled wildly because what the man was talking about was too interesting to even consider fathoming.

This man got pieced off and requested that he leave his home because nobody can choose for him. At any rate, I don't fault him. It very well may be one of those side effects of advanced age. This man said he wouldn't let this marriage thing of dig disturb his timetables for the year so he gave a date that won't incline toward my chief. I argued for a change however he as expected rejected it. He simply could have done without anything about me. I used to feel that it was just ladies that exhibit such ways of behaving yet my in-regulation changed my discernment. He never permitted me to go into Gift's space to try and visit with her since he said until I wed her, I can't go near her.

We just arranged a conventional wedding. I came to illuminate my supervisor about the date and he said I shouldn't stress, he will reschedule a portion of his exercises so he sets aside a few minutes for me. Well, I generally accept the maxim that God isn't the man to lie nor are our ways his methodologies. Whenever He has composed something about you, He will find available resources of causing you to accomplish it. Simply take a gander at how somebody I know from nowhere possesses energy for me whiles my blood relations dismissed me. Assuming a man rejects you, your dad in paradise rejects you not. I just got myself another family.

My supervisor requested that I go back to my town and welcome my family members to come and observe the function for me. I let him know that was excessive because they never so that once considered searching for me might check whether am as yet alive or dead. I let him know his family and about a couple of companions are enough for me. I did not at all like greeting cards too. Gee, upon the arrival of the wedding function, Gift's dad said he was not feeling well overall.

My companions who came to observe the program were situated, Gift's family were likewise present barring her dad. This man guaranteed he was having stomach torment so we ought to give him time. He approached the scene of the service neither did he go to the emergency clinic. We endlessly trusted that this man will come yet he wasn't coming. His significant other went into his room just to find her better half practically biting the dust. She began yelling at top of her voice so we as a whole suspected this man was dead. I went inside to see what was happening just so that I might see this man battling to breathe. I immediately requested his vehicle keys and hurried him to the medical clinic. Every one of these whiles, our visitors were situated sitting tight for us.

I let the medical caretakers know that we want his presence in the house gravely. They said we ought to ask for his condition to balance out quicker. After approximately a couple of hours at the emergency clinic, my to-be in-regulation recaptured his cognizance. He was given some energy sponsor and was informed his family needs his attendance at the house so he ought to return home and after the program, he ought to get back to an emergency clinic for audit. He said there was no requirement for him to return home since what was happening in his home was not to his desire.

We begged this man until he acknowledged to go with us. I was only upset for my visitors who came promptly in the first part of the day and were holding up till that time. Some of them couldn't stand by longer so they left. We got to the house around 4:00 pm. Because of this, we want to quickly wrap the program up request for early completion. One of the older men chipping away at my supervisor's building went about as my dad and my manager's significant other went about as my mom. At the point when it got to the piece of the program where we expected to introduce the things, my in-regulation asked where her girl's vehicle was and he was unable to see the parents-in-law's fuel recompense as well as a few other entertaining things he composed. Her significant other who was my mother by marriage acted the hero and said I told her we will bring them later. This man said since her better half was taking choices for his benefit, she ought to go on with the remainder of the program. He lashed out and went into his room. Everyone around began talking against this man. Gift let him know that he was shaming himself as well as her. Truly, the service was no good thing to think of home about. We effectively addressed something and later, I took my significant other and child with me.

wonder went with us to assist Gift with looking after the children. She has finished secondary school so was free at home. At the point when we returned home, my supervisor gave us an extra room where supernatural occurrences could remain. Two days after that sparse commitment, wonder came to me one night while her sister was resting in the room. She said she was upset about what occurred among us furthermore, she wasn't in a decent mental state so I ought to pardon her. She said it was crafted by Satan. Indeed, Satan ought to quit pestering individuals so they quit accusing him regardless of whether he exists.

"wonder, I have nothing against you except to ensure you don't rehash such off-kilter conduct in this house. You are a lot mindful that this isn't my home so, with the easily overlooked detail you do, we can be conveyed." I told her. She expressed gratitude toward me and went into her room. I never permitted the open door given to me to change my way of behaving.

I proceeded with my work in the house not surprisingly. In the first part of the day, I will convey my supervisor's significant other to school and when she shut, I will in any case go for her. Regardless of her bliss being hitched to my chief, she had a profound struggle. Her concern was that her significant other needed more time for her. This is my recommendation to the women that need to wed such rich men since they won't have any desire to free their monetary status, they work harder and that makes it challenging for them to remain at home. So assuming you are hitched to them be ready to appreciate living alone when he isn't anywhere near.

Particularly those of them doing global organizations. Scarcely will my manager spend an entire week at home. Today he is going for this gathering, tomorrow he is voyaging, tomorrow next he is expected to go to a meeting, and so on. It was his bustling timetables that made him like me that much since I was generally there for him. The adoration among myself and Gift was additionally developing great and anybody that perceives how we focused on one another wants to get hitched. the supernatural occurrence was additionally in the house doing the looking after children.

Gift acquired work at some country bank in our space so that additionally expanded the requirement for marvel to keep on remaining with us. After exactly a couple of months, marvel began showing her underhanded part to my chief. Normally she is delightful and there were no two different ways about that. My manager began having an interest in her to the degree that he doesn't focus on his better half any longer. I understood that supernatural occurrence began wearing extremely short skirts and dresses that uncovered her delicate parts.

Lady Faustina likewise saw this and requested that I converse with her. Lady was additionally starting to have interest in me since her better half cannot deal with her. One evening, the lady called me from school and said she wasn't feeling great so I ought to come and bring her back home. Gift additionally went to work so it was left with marvel and Olorunsogo the Junior.

My manager as expected was nowhere to be found and his dad likewise includes an alternate level inside a similar structure. I went for the lady and on the way, she got a few prescriptions to fix her cerebral pain. At the point when we got to the house, she said she was extremely feeble so I ought to convey her on my back into her room. "Lady please wonder if could think something happening between us would it be advisable for her she sees this." I shared it with her.

"Okay sit back and relax. Simply assist me with my pack to the room." She mentioned. I took the pack and followed her into the room. "Agbanavor might you at any point read what is happening inside me?" She asked when we got into the room. "Lady please how?" I inquired. "Come and allow me to clear up for you. Come why? is it true or not that you fear coming near me? She inquired. I strolled towards her and this woman got me with an embrace. " Agbanvor ensure you kill this inclination inside me before leaving this room." She said with an exceptionally heartfelt voice.

Will Olorunsogo disregard his past unexpectedly early? Did Miracle see what was happening? What next?

Chapter 2

Madam please with all due respect, what you are expecting me to do will be the worse thing I will ever do in this world. I was lost when Mr Charles came to find me, this shouldn't be the right way of paying him back. Please let's not do this." I begged her" Olorunsogo am actually dying inside. You leaving me alone will be more than killing me slowly. Your boss won't know about this and I will make sure I provide all your needs including your wife's. Just help me. Okay I will give you Ghc1000.00 as soon as we are done."

She held me by my waist whiles saying that. "Madam please I won't do it. Leave me alone to go. If you try pushing me to the wall, I will report you to my boss and you know what that will mean." I said to her. "Hey my friend don't even try it. Now you have to do this or else I will shout and say you want to rape me and you equally know what that will mean." She said back.

Hmm just as my boss said, as a strong man, you will be faced with challenges, problems and setbacks but what makes the difference is how you are able to discipline yourself and overcome them. The voice that set me moving from my village also said life is full of choices, at every point in life's journey, one has to make a choice and every choice also has its implications. Yes I needed money to be independent and also self sufficient but not through an evil means such as this. How could I sleep with my own boss's wife?

To be honest, this challenge was too tough for me to bare. It was through the same means that sent me out of my formal house and made my in-law hate me for life. If my in-law on earth should hate me for life, what then will God in heaven do? Am even not sure I will be judged before pushed into hell fire. "Madam please you know what you want us to do is against the will of God?" I asked.

She remained silent and burst into tears. She went to sleep on her bed with her face bowed on the bed and cried more. "Madam please what is it? Why are you crying?" I asked. "Please I wish you could leave me alone inside. I want some privacy. " she said. "Okay sorry if I've offended you." I walked out of her room. You could see from my shirt that the room was warm so I was frightened what anyone that will see me coming out of the room will suspect and this was because when we entered, she didn't switch on the air condition. Immediately I stepped out, this was miracle standing by the wall leading to madam's room.

Me: miracle why are you standing here?

miracle: Olorunsogo you've done well. But why are you sweating like this?

Me: why are you saying I've done well? I asked feeling guilty.

miracle: No need explaining anything. I overhead everything that went on inside. I'm only standing here to congratulate you.

Me: and what do you mean by that?

miracle: I didn't say you did anything wrong. Don't let your conscience deceive you. Am congratulating you on how you were able to deal with that tough Olympic tournament. I was in my room when I saw both of you going into her room so I suspected something hahaha. Oh but you've done well. My sister must be grateful for having you.

Me: hmm so miracle tell me why you ladies are like that? It was through this same means that I got your sister pregnant. You also tried it on me and now madam. Why?

miracle: haha are you telling me your history? Look, don't think it is only you men that has feelings and chase after ladies. We equally have and it's even stronger than what you guys experience. When it comes, we find our own ways and means of satisfying ourselves. So when we have any available man around, why won't we take advantage. I understand madam, her husband feels he can just marry such a beautiful woman like that and leave her at home to suffer. He thinks body is firewood.

Me: hmm really? Then I will suggest to you that it's not the best. You people need deliverance. Where is my boy?

.

miracle: He is asleep.

I walked with her to see Olorunsogo the Junior sleeping soundly. I thanked God I didn't push further for the abortion of the pregnancy. I went back to continue with my daily routines in the house. In the process, I thought about what just happened. If we thought what happened in that room was a secret between myself and madam but someone saw it long ago, then am sure God even saw the end before it started.

Thank God I took the right decision. Soon my wife returned from work and there was joy in the house. Madam was just not in her normal mood for the rest of the day. All she did was to join us take supper and returned to her room. miracle also played her role well by not making madam know that she was aware of what went on.

The following day, on our way to alight madam at her school, she apologized for what happened. "Agbanavor, am sorry for what happened yesterday, I actually don't know what came over me. Please forgive me." "Oh madam, you need not to be worried. I understand you very well. I think it will be good if you could explain things to your husband about how you do miss him when he is away, I think he can readjust his schedules so that he could equally have time for you." I said.

"Hmm my brother, you should even be asking why till now I've not gotten pregnant. My husband has never satisfied me for once. It is barely seven months now since we got married. You won't understand." She said looking very worried. "Madam I understand everything you said. I will help you overcome all your difficulties." I said to her.

"And what do you think you can do to help me?" She asked. "Don't worry, it will be in-between me and boss." I said to her. Soon we got to her school and I returned home. Everything in the house seemed to stabilize for some time until my boss returned from America. Per what madam was telling me in the car the other time, it seems my boss was not performing well in bed. This added to the reasons for him not staying home. Haha it could also mean madam's libidinal energy was higher than my boss could take. I thanked God I didn't try it for her to break my spine. On our way to inspect progress of his building project, I tried in my own way to find out if madam's claims were true.

Me: eei boss but so soon do you know you are almost getting a year old after your wedding ceremony?

Boss: Yes oo my guy, time is flying like a bird.

Me: but till now madam is still not carrying belly. Or are you waiting to complete your building before you hit harder? Haha

Boss: hahaha bad boy, that was what you did and impregnated someone's daughter. Hmm guy but on a more serious note you did well oo, yeah because it's not easy impregnating a lady. I've been doing all I should do but the pregnancy is still not coming.

Me: oh really! Okay boss let me see how best I can help you. You know am a village boy and know more about herbs. I will get you some to be taking and I assure you that sooner or later, she will beg you to stop and the next thing you will see is pregnancy.

Boss: are you serious with what you are saying? Like I will be forever thankful to you.

I assured him. I went into some forest close to the site to search for the herbs I will use for the medicines for him. It wasn't any big forest but it was more than a simple bush. Suddenly, I heard a voice telling me to look back. I turned and there was nothing behind me. I kept moving forward searching for the herbs.

I was not finding the particular one I was looking for. I heard the voice again telling me to look back. All this while, the voice was saying I should take note of where

I passed before reaching where I got to in the forest. I didn't notice that. I got to the middle of the forest and now, I couldn't locate my way back again. I also saw the particular herb this time around but where to pass and go back became the problem. I will come and appear at where I started in the forest.

Time was far spent so my boss became worried for me not returning. He sent his boys to come into the forest and look for me. As soon as they started their search, I fell into a trance. In the trance, I saw the image I saw back in my village before leaving, and it said to me, "My son let your sister in-law leave the house before you give the herb to your boss if not she will make you loose everything."

I came into consciousness when I heard a loud voice mentioning my name, it was the voice of the people searching for me. I responded so they were able to trace my voice and came to rescue me. I told them I lost my way out. I apologized to my boss for keeping him waiting. He said he was rather scared something happened to me. I showed the herbs to him but didn't tell him what went on in the forest. This time around, I ignored the voice because miracle was helping her sister. My boy too was growing well.

I dried the herb for one full week. I then asked him to use it as bitters. My number is xxxxxxxx call me let me get some of the herb for you. My boss started taking this medicine and come see things for yourself. For two and a half hours, he was still active. Just as I knew, he cancelled some of his business schedules and stayed at home. One afternoon, he sent me to the site to check something for him, his wife was gone to work, my wife also went to work. My boss's father traveled so basically it was left with miracle, my son and my boss. miracle took advantage of the situation. She seduced my boss and because my boss has his vitality drug under his bed, he used it and serviced miracle very well.

They became secret lovers and were doing their own thing in the dark. This time around, madam was suspecting her husband against miracle. One night, Charles woke up quietly to miracle' room. They started having affair when madam woke up and realized her husband was not beside her on the bed. She started looking for him. First she checked the wash room but Charles was not there.

She decided to check the kitchen and from their room to the kitchen, you need to pass in front of my room. When she got to my entrance, she heard a loud moaning from Gift and that increased her quest to look for her husband. She went into the kitchen and still Charles wasn't around. Something prompted her to check miracle' room. Lo and behold, the moaning from my room was even nothing compared to the one from miracle' room.

The one miracle was giving was very loud so my boss was cautioning her to stop making noise. This was where madam nearly went mad. She pushed the door and it was locked. She knocked and miracle came out in a towel to open the door. Madam didn't ask her anything before slapping her very loud in the face. She pushed her away from the door and entered the room. Charles quickly went to hide himself inside the wardrobe in the room.

"Where is my husband you stupid girl?" Madam asked. Before she could say additional words, miracle also replied with a heavy slap. It turned into a fight between madam and miracle. My boss realizing where the thing was getting to wouldn't help, he came out in his boxers to separate them. Madam got more furious and took some champagne bottle on the table to break miracle' head but luckily for her, my boss used his hands to block the bottle in the air but got a very deep cut in the end.

miracle also wanted to use another bottle on madam and this time around, because of the pain my boss was going through, he couldn't save the bottle this time around, it landed on her heard and straight, madam went into coma. This was when Charles rushed to call me to help him. By then I was also just warming up for my next round when he came to call. I opened the door only to see him bleeding seriously. I asked what happened to him and he said it was nothing so I should help his wife. I was running towards his room when he redirected me to miracle' room. I got in and madam was lying restlessly on the floor. miracle was standing there with the towel on and looking at her without any concern.

"miracle what is happening?" I asked. She was pointing at me with the remaining broken bottle. "Stop asking me questions if not you will receive your part of it." She said. "What has come over you? Are you getting insane?" I asked. "You are rather getting insane." She threw the bottle at me but I dodged it. I carried madam and was sending her into the car so that we rush her to the hospital. Come and see trouble for me. Due to anxiety, I was holding the car keys in my hand but was still looking for it in the room.

What has come over miracle? Will madam survive?

Chapter 3

Gift please haven't you seen where I left the car keys?" I asked. "Sweetheart is that not the key in your hands?" Gift responded. I gave myself a knock on my head and dashed off the room. Gift helped clean the blood from Charles my boss but he said he was okay. He tied it with a bandage and decided to go with me to the hospital. He quickly went to his room and wore some clothes and without delay, we sped to the hospital.

The nurses came out and with a sense of eagerness and responsibility, took madam to the emergency unit and fixed oxygen on her. The doctor came around and prompted the need to put her on life support machine. Actually, the strength at which miracle smashed the bottle on her was very severe. My boss was also losing more blood. The bandage was soaked with blood and this drew the attention of the nurses.

He was also admitted and due to the blood loss, they needed to infuse him with pints of blood. He was given more than six packs of blood because he was also gradually becoming unconscious. The doctor came few minutes after. They dressed his wounds and sent him to the male ward where he was admitted. After the atmosphere looked a bit calm, the doctor called me to his office.

Doctor: so what exactly happened in the house?

Me: Doc. I can't vividly tell how everything started. I'm their driver as well as the caretaker of their house. I was in my room when suddenly I heard a knock on my door this night. I came out only to see my boss bleeding so I thought probably there were some robbers around. I asked what the problem was but he refused to tell me. He only directed me to go help his wife in one of the rooms. I went and saw madam motionless on the floor. So quickly I rushed the two of them here.

Doctor: alright. I think this will need the concern of the police because something might be wrong somewhere.

Me: Oh I don't think there is the need now. Please attend to them to get well first before we find the cause. I want them alive because apart from God, they are my life.

Doctor: alright don't worry they will be fine.
Y
I knew that when I should allow him to involve the police, miracle would definitely be made to face the full rigours of the law. Around 2pm that day, Mr Charles gained consciousnesses fully. He was discharged but madam was still in a critical condition. He was allowed

to go and see her in the emergency room. I went with him and this was where he became furious with miracle. “I can’t believe this is my wife, I am going to skin miracle alive.” He said. The doctor asked him what happened.

“Doctor there is a devil in my house. She caused all this.” He said but I pretended I had no idea about what went on. He was able to narrate what went on but didn’t add what he went doing in miracle’ room at the time. The doctor made him sign a claim form which was sent to the police. Back home, Gift cooked breakfast in the morning for us but we were not coming.

She went to check on miracle only to see her lying on the floor. She called out her name to see if she was okay. miracle woke up and started chasing her sister with a broken bottle. Luckily for my wife, together with the police, we arrived at the house and saw what was happening. The police managed to get hold of her and handcuffed her. My boss told the police miracle was responsible for the troubles in the house. They took her away and detained her behind bars for further investigations.

My boss’s father came to hear about what was going on and ordered the police to arrest all of us. He described what happened as a conspiracy against his son. He claimed we wanted to kill his son and take over his properties. The worse was my innocent wife who had no idea and my small boy. The Police came for all of us and locked us in a cell. My boss's father was a public figure and very influential in the area so the police acted on his orders. The officer In charge of criminal investigation ordered his men to torture me so that I tell the truth. I was beaten and hurt with the flames of a candle. They minimized the torture on my wife because she was still breastfeeding the baby.

After thorough investigations, my wife and son was allowed to go home but preparations was made for miracle and I to face the court of law. miracle started behaving strangely in the cell. She talked to herself and clapped to something no one could see nor hear. The police suggested they refer her to the Psychiatric hospital for assessment. When she was taken there, it was proven that she was experiencing Mania (A mental illness marked by periods of excitement, delusions and over activity).

After few weeks that Charles, my boss realized I had no idea about what went on, he told his father to let the police release me. His father was of the view that, he shouldn't entertain us in his house again. He then told his father what exactly went on and that he was the primary cause of everything because if he were not to snick out his wife, nothing as such could have happened. But he agreed not to allow miracle into the house. I equally blamed myself for the cause of the trouble because I should've obeyed the voice I heard in the forest by asking miracle out of the house before I gave the medicine to my boss.

Eventually, they came to release us from the cell. I bet you, I wouldn't recommend the cell to any innocent soul. Life in there was mini hell. I wouldn't want to describe what I saw there because it was an eyesore. Gift felt sorry for me and hated her sister for life. I advised her not to because it wasn't her making. It was her mental condition that made her do all that she did. As indicated, the condition poses the individual to be very excited at times and do things he/she wouldn't have done when in her normal state hence miracle seducing men when it comes. They also do have delusions and becomes over active at times hence miracle chasing her own sister with the bottle.

I thanked my boss for ordering our release. I thanked his father too but he made it known he was not ready for a caretaker anymore so he insisted I pack and leave the house within two months. He said once miracle was able to do such a thing, he feared the condition is in their generic makeup so he is obvious the situation might repeat itself. Madam was already responding to treatment. What my boss did was he gave me money to rent another place where I could stay with my wife and son.

Luckily too, we got a place which was not far from where Gift works. miracle was also receiving treatment but we were fined to pay a huge sum of money before the case could be dismissed. The police explained that they would've imprisoned miracle for what she did but because she was diagnosed as a Psychiatric patient, she was charged to pay Ghc5000.00. It wasn't fair to me though. If my boss were not to go into the room, that wouldn't have happened.

When Gift's father heard of what went on, he said it served us right. He also blamed me for miracle' condition and due to this, he refused to pay the money. We were also given two weeks to pay the money and if not I will be held responsible since miracle was seen to be mentally ill. The medical bills my boss also needed to pay was very high. He needed to pay this money in order to save her life. I explained to my boss to help me pay for the court fines but unfortunately for me this time around, he said he was hard up. His building project must even be put on hibernation for sometime. I then asked Gift to help me pay for that money since she was also working.

Out of love for me and her sister, she took all she had in her account and I added all I had but yet still, it wasn't up to the amount. I needed to borrow from some friends to add up. I fortunately got the money and paid for the case to be dismissed. I've now come to class one again. We moved out of the house to our newly rented apartment. Thankfully, madam was discharged but could not remember anything that happened. It even took her days to recognize her husband.

Now that I lost my source of income, my father in-law had a good standing to take Gift away from me despite the fact that I married her. Anytime Gift visited them, his main focus was that she should divorce me. miracle was also doing well on medication. Gift always stood firm that she loved me and nothing will make her leave me. She explained to her father that, love was not all about money.

“Daddy am not complaining in my matrimonial home. Besides, my husband doesn’t come begging for food from you before we eat. He loves me and I love him too. It is your daughter, miracle who is to be blamed for his financial handicap. I have the peace I want so Daddy with due respect, I am not leaving my husband alone. For better for worse, in riches or poverty, we will love each other. Just look at my son, is he not growing well? Daddy please reconsider your decisions” miracle said to her father. “Alright, well Said. I wish you the best.” Her father said. Gift thanked him and left.

After two years of treatment, miracle’ condition became stabilized. Most people feel mental illnesses cannot be cured. That is not really true. With continues medication and good enabling environment, the situation can stabilize and the person will be good to go but it also depends on the severity of the condition. miracle came back into her normal state and luckily for her, gained admission into the university to study Political science.

I also got employed by one pure water factory to be the driver for one of their vans so I may say life was manageable for us until I was involved in an accident.

Hmm to be a man is not just a matter of being a male but being able to face challenges. The accident affected my reproductive organ so what happened to my boss was gradually eating into myself and Gift.

Will Gift change towards the man she loved?

Chapter 4

Gift started behaving strangely towards me. She goes to work and comes back late. If I try complaining, she will only give some flimsy excuses. She was even the one who found the job as a driver for me. The sachet water factory belongs to her boss so when she explained things to him concerning my unemployment status and her boss gave me the opportunity to drive one of his vans.

When the accident occurred, the factory footed the bill to some point and stopped. How I wished I had an insurance cover by then. The accident inflicted terrible pains on my spinal cord such that, I needed to undergo a surgery.

I had to accumulate money to continue the surgery in order to correct the problem but the money was no where to be found. We used all we had to pay the court charges. When it's night, I do feel the pain in my spinal cord so there was no way I could have sex with my wife. Initially she was able to cope with the situation but as time went on, she started putting up this behaviour.

One interesting thing we don't usually recognize is that, some behaviours can show a partner is cheating but might not necessarily be. Indications and suspicions does not always mean cheating. If you don't have a definitive proof of your wife cheating, don't let your suspicion carry you away and make accusations of infidelity. Be very sure of your facts before you draw conclusions, if not, you will just be building up pressure in your heart.

Anyway, I think trust for each other also matters. What I'm saying doesn't mean you should wait until everything is out of hand before you take action. All I'm saying is have enough facts and don't put yourself into any unnecessary pressure. One evening, Faustina asked me how long I will remain in my condition instead of making her feel like a woman

Me: Gift, I know how you are feeling. Don't worry. I will be okay very soon. I know how much you love me. Help me raise money to complete the surgery."

Gift: My husband, I believe that you will be fine. I do feel bad seeing you like this. Don't worry. I will ask my father to help us.

Me: Your father? No. Please don't multiply the problems. How can you go to your father asking him to help us? I don't agree with you

Gift: I'm going as his daughter and not the wife of his enemy. I don't believe my father will listen to me and refuse to help us. He loves me and will be ready to do everything for me to be happy. You just leave everything to me.

Me: Hmm I'm just foreseeing danger ahead of me should you go to this man for help. I think we should rather check from Charles and his wife.

Gift: Yes that is not a bad idea.

A week later, she went to Charles' house but unfortunately, he wasn't in the country. She met his wife, Madam Faustina, only in the house. Madam Faustina expressed her wish to help but due to what happened, all their money was used to settle the hospital bills. She said she was not sure her husband could equally help. Gift came back to tell me about how it went. I felt bad but there was nothing I could do. I wouldn't say madam Faustina was wicked to us because we were all aware how much money was spent on her to bring her back to life. Gift suggested I start going to church and probably, the church could help raise funds for me. I explained to her that was not a good idea because going to church shouldn't be on a condition that I needed some material help from them.

This has almost being the mindset of some people in church. They attend church because they want some material help from them. Yes, the church is more or less a society where there is the need for mutual support for one another but that shouldn't be the main motive for going to church. We go to church simply to worship God together as a group in order to secure our salvation. I agreed to join a church but not because of the help I needed. Few weeks later, Gift sneaked out of the house to her father's house.

She was supposed to pick Junior Olorunsogo from school that day but she didn't. She thought she could return before they close from school. She went to tell her father what was happening to me and requested for his help. My in-law just stood up and went into his room after Gift has finished saying what she had to say. He never uttered a word before going into his room. Gift was thinking he was going to probably take his cheque book to sign for her. She waited for long but he wasn't coming out. She decided to check on him at the room and saw him sitting by his table reading a news paper.

Gift: Dad I told you something but you never responded. I have been waiting for you to come and give me a response but you were not coming so I decide to follow up.

Dad: Do I look like a Father Christmas to you? Or have you heard in the news that your father has started operating some charity organization?

Gift: oh Dad please it hasn't gotten to that. Remember I'm still your daughter.

Dad: My daughter my foot. My daughter will listen to my advice and take instructions from me. My daughter will not feel like she knows better than her father. My daughter won't marry any good for nothing idiot like what you call your husband. Lady, you can see I'm reading on issues concerning this country and beyond. I wish you leave me to continue reading.

Gift: I want to believe you won't feel bad when something happens to me. I will fight for my husband and I know you will one day see miracles happen for us. I'm leaving.

Dad: Don't forget to close the door after you.

Her father said to her and with tears she went out. Gift thought her father had a change of mind when he called her back. "Come I have something good for you." Her father said. Gift eagerly returned and got closer to her father. "Take that brown envelope on the bed for me", her father requested. Gift went to take it for him and he asked her to sit down. All these while, Gift's phone was off. She knew I will call so she switched it off.

Her father took the envelope and brought out a magazine. It was a magazine belonging to his network marketing company. He opened it and showed her a picture of one gentleman who was earning Ghc 3000.00 per week. He said that guy was still single and wanted a beautiful but intelligent lady to marry. "I told him I will give one of my daughters to him to marry.

Precisely, I was referring to your younger sister. But looking at things, I can see you are not having any happiness in that thing you call marriage so I wanted to give you to him. Forget about that gateman. He has no future for you" Her Dad said.

Gift: Daddy I think we are coming back to class one. I told you severally that I don't want any other man than Olorunsogo. Please let miracle get married to him and I'm sure you will be very excited to see your daughter marrying a millionaire. For me I'm out.

This time around, she never asked any permission but left the room. She looked at the wall clock in the hall and time was far gone. "Oh my God, Junior will still be waiting for me at school", she said to herself. She switched on her phone this time around and called to informed me that something went wrong somewhere so she will come and tell me later. She asked me to call someone to go in for Junior from school because, by the time she will get there, it will be too late. I told her I already called the school so one of his teachers brought him to the house.

Gift came to narrate everything that happened in her father's house to me. I queried her that I had warned her not to go there but she didn't listen. She apologized and prepared supper for the home. As the days and weeks went past, my condition was just getting severe. I now found it difficult to even sit down. My better position was to lie on the bed. Gift was having the feeling that it won't be long and I will die if no action was taken. She said she wouldn't like to be called a widow at her tender age.

One day when she got to work, she decided to ask her boss who was the owner of the factory I worked with to support her in flying me out of the country for the surgery. Her boss said she should come to his house after work for any amount of her choice because he could feel the pain she was going through. Gift thanked her stars and even praised her boss with more bootlicking words. After work, Gift went for Junior at school and sent him home. She then said she had some appointment at her work side so she will join us later and left to this man's house.

Mr Mike, her boss, was equally married but he cheats on his wife. He was sometime ago reported contracted some STI but I was not very sure of that. That very day, his wife was not around at the time Gift got there. He gave her a warm reception and later, brought out his cheque book and asked Gift to write any amount she wants on the cheque so that he signs for her.

Gift wrote Ghc50,000.00 and handed the cheque back to him. Mr Mike saw the amount and smiled. "Gift all this money will be yours on just one condition" He said. The condition was Gift to satisfy him sexually that evening and any other time he requested for it. He placed the cheque on the center table and sat down. "Use what you have to get what you want", He said.

Chapter 5

What do you mean Mr Mike? I should give myself to you before you help me treat my husband who had an accident whiles driving your own van?" "Hey! Madam don't go there. The company compensated your husband as our working conditions stated so don't try to say we have ignored him. I've given you the only option available. Take it or leave it", Mr Mike sounded a bit angry. "I'm highly disappointed in you", Gift said as tears rolled down her cheeks.

Madam there is no need crying or being disappointed in me. You allowing me access to what is under your dress will not take anything away from you. If you keep your mouth shut on what will go on now, no one will know about it. You've got a fresh skin so stop living your holy life here and let's get going.

I will be in my room, when you are ready, just open the door and enter", he said as he took the cheque from the table and went into his bedroom. The decision became very tough for Gift this time around. Letting a cheque of Ghc50,000.00 go simply because she held strongly to her moral intelligence and seeing her beloved husband die due to poverty seemed challenging to let it happen. Gift sat down with tears flowing like a stream of water.

Back in the house, I was contemplating of what kind of meeting will be going on which kept Gift out of home for so long. It didn't look normal because, even on days they needed to close the company's end of year account, they did it within working hours. I called her number which went through but she didn't pick up. I called one of her colleagues to find out, if truly, a meeting was going on. The lady I contacted said she was on leave but assured me she will enquire about it and report back to me.

In a few minutes, she called back and said there was no such meeting. I wondered why should my wife would lie to me. "She will come and meet me today", I said to her colleague over the phone as if I had the strength to do something. She pleaded with me to take it easy with her when she comes back.

Gift went deep into herself and said "God, please tell me what to do. My husband needs money to come back into his normalcy. I love him and don't want him dead now. Please forgive me if I commit this sin to save a life". Looking at the time, she realised she has exhaused most of her time so she needed to take a decision and move on. What Gift was trying to do was just similar to what Jesus Christ came to do for us. Because of the love he had for us, he sacrificed his life for us to have life, he took the position of a sinner just to make us righteous, he was tortured just to make us free. Gift had to make a choice this dying moment.

She walked with calculated steps and face filled with tears into Mr Mike's bedroom. "Here I am. Use me for anything so that I can save my husband's life", she said to Mr Mike who was already in his boxers lying on his bed. "Young lady, why are you doing things as if I want to kill you? How can we enjoy ourselves when you are crying? Please if you are not ready, am not forcing you, just leave", Mr Mike said sounding very authoritative.

Gift unfastened the button of her dress, took it off leaving her bra and trousers. "Wow! You have beautiful breasts, let me help you open the bra". Mr Mike stood up with his elongated stick. He gave Gift a hug and unlocked her bra. Gift was actually not having any feeling for all that he was doing. Mr Mike removed her trousers and pushed her to the bed. Gift was almost naked. She was only left in her under wear. Mr Mike started massaging her in order to get her activated.

Gradually, Gift was coming into the game. She asked Mr Mike if he had condoms, but Mike ignored that question. God in his knowledge does things just to help us from such situations. It was true that Mr Mike was a carrier of HIV/AIDS. He was on anti retroviral drugs. Due to this, he stopped having sex with his wife from the day he was tested positive. Luckily for his wife, she was negative. Mr Mike had this infection out of the promiscuous life he was living but to his continuous medication, he still looked very active.

That is one benefit of HIV drugs. They are able to sustain your CD4 count with the help of good diet, rest and an enabling environment. Gift attended a workshop where they were taught of some of these drugs people take. Among them are Lamivudine and Tenofovir Disoproxil Fumarate tablets. Mr Mike had his Lamivudine on a stool beside the bed. Gift's gaze landed on this medicine and asked Mr Mike to give her a few seconds. She went straight to take the tablet and examined it.

Mr Mike: But what are you doing with that medicine? Or do you also need some?

Gift: Who does this medicine belong to?

Mr Mike: My friend stop asking questions and let's enjoy ourselves. Your sick guy should be waiting for you.

Gift: Are you HIV positive?

Mr Mike: But how can you ask me such a question? How can you come to my house and be asking me if I'm HIV positive?

Gift: This medicine is given to such people. Mr Mike don't hide this from me. You are HIV positive.

Mr Mike: eerm my dear I can explain.

Gift: explain what?

Mr Mike: please it is only my wife and my doctor who knows about my condition. Yes I am HIV positive but mine is not transferrable.

Gift: you are very wicked Mr Mike. You knew you were in this condition and yet still you wanted to sleep with me. God will punish you. The whole world will hear about this.

Mr Mike: what did you just say?

Gift: Yes the whole world will know what you are doing. I wonder the number of ladies you've shared the virus to. From that lady, she will give it her husband or other people, and from those people, it will spread and cover the whole community. I will call for your arrest.

Mr Mike: Gift please don't do such a thing. I will be disgraced. Please keep this secret between just the two of us. Okay, let me sign the cheque for you. I will also promote you at work so that you keep this as a secret.

Gift: hmm you are very funny. You giving me HIV which will be for the life time and eventually leading me to early grave is better than the disgrace you will go through isn't it? Add Ghc10.000.00 to the amount I wrote on the cheque and sign it for me. I will keep it as a secret.

Mr Mike quickly took his cheque booklet and signed a new cheque of Ghc60,000.00 for her. Gift dressed up and left the room. The only thing I was not sure of is if they kissed. Kissing was also seen as a risk behaviour to getting the infection from an infected person but it is not a hundred percent must that you kissing an infected person should guarantee you to get the disease. We men at times don't have patience for our wives. As I said earlier, we won't wait for them to explain themselves to us before we start rattling.

She got to the house around 8pm. By then, Junior was asleep but I was still awake waiting for her. I was just wondering how I would skin her alive when she came.

Me: How was the meeting?

Gift: oh sweetheart it went well.

Me: oh what is that on your face? Come closer let me remove it for you.

Immediately she got closer I slapped her very hard to the extent than I felt a severe pain at my back.

Me: how dare you lie to me? Where are you coming from?

She remained silent and held her jaw. "I said where are you coming from? I called your colleague and I was told no meeting has been called. So where are you coming from?" I asked again. She poured out a lot of blood as she opened her mouth. The slap made her to bite her tongue and lips. Her face got swollen. Little did I know my anger was about to complicate issues. She dropped her bag and with pain, a bleeding mouth and tears, went into the washroom to clean the blood.

She left the bag behind so I managed to pick it and something pushed me to check inside. Lo and behold, I saw the cheque of Ghc60,000.00 which was dated for the next day. I checked the name used to sign it and it was her boss. Gift came back into the room in tears and said, "I nearly killed myself because of you. I nearly sent myself into hell because of you. I nearly destroyed my family because of you. You couldn't have little patience for me so that I tell you where I was coming from. All you did was to shout at me and slap me. You've caused me pain". I was really touched by what she said. "Dear I'm very sorry. I know I've gone too far. Please I promise this will never happen again", I pleaded. She didn't say anything. She then narrated how she went to her boss to ask for money which she could use to treat me. She said she has planned sending me overseas for the surgery. I thanked her and also apologized for what I did.

She was not able to go to work the following day because her swollen face. She needed to cover her face even before taking her small boy to school. She seeked permission from her boss and she was given three days off.

Three days later, she went to cash out the money only for her to be told that, her boss recently transferred all he had in that account into another account so there was nothing to be given to her. They rejected the cheque. She went to her boss at his office and threatened to report her to the police station before he signed a different cheque for her.

So had it not being because of the secret, he would've just slept with my wife for free because, same would have happened if she tries to cash the cheque. She came back to the house with the money and she took me back to the hospital where they first attended to me. They said they will transfer him to Cuba where the surgery could be done. They gave me some treatment and said they will prepare the papers and let me go in two weeks.

On Sunday within the week, Gift went to church and her pastor told her that her husband's condition can only be corrected through prayers. She came home with her pastor and some other members. They came to pray for me. After the prayer, the pastor said in few days, we will see miracles. With faith, we shouted a big Amen. The date for my transfer was due so I reported to the hospital so that the procedure could continue.

The doctor said they needed to take an x-ray scan to attach to the documents that will be added to my referral letter. Miraculously, the doctor examined the result and said there will be the need for another one. They did it for three consecutive times and said the bones has been positioned where it was supposed to be so there will be no need for me going to Cuba. This is the kind of God we serve. He works in miracles and indeed with Christ in you, there will be hope of glory. I was to remain on admission for some days so that they correct everything. Few days after I was discharged from the hospital, we heard the news that miracle was pregnant for one of her lecturers on campus.

This shouldn't be a surprise because a behaviour once formed is difficult to change. Her father called for the abortion of the pregnancy so that she could marry the man he planned for her. miracle equally agreed with her father and abortion was done successfully at the hospital. They arranged the actual marriage for her and the rich man. Their kind of wedding was very memorial.

My father in-law was very happy that day. He wore an expensive cloth to portray his joy for his daughter. The number of cars that were present was uncountable. Despite I was not very fit, I was able to impress Gift a bit and she was okay with it. The money she got was from Mr Mike was given to me to start up a business. Gift is actually the love of my life.

Chapter 6

I'm not sure I will ever get any other lady that can be very supportive and submissive to her husband like that. The money was used to start up a boutique business manned by me as she did her job. Her colleagues were surprised when they realized Gift was recommended for promotion. She was recommended to be the branch manager as her boss was to be relocated to their national office to work till he becomes a pensioner, which will be four years later.

Actually, there were other staff more qualified than her for that promotion but because of personal interests, Mr Mike gave her that opportunity. Soon, she became the branch manager. There were whole lots of oppressions by some authorities to disqualify her but all proved futile.

Gift was naturally beautiful, smart and intelligent so she even would've been selected before other staff. "Our financial life has actually been catapulted from nowhere to somewhere. Thanks to Mr Mike. Yes I need to thank him because he was the reason for this breakthrough. They may plan evil against you but God will rather turn everything to your benefit. Mr Mike had wanted to infest us with HIV but God turned it into our financial breakthrough", said Gift

After their expensive wedding, miracle went back to campus and instead of quitting the relationship with the lecturer who impregnated her, she continued. She had a simple reason to that because this lecturer happened to be their exams officer for her department. When individual lecturers submit their end of semester results, he will conspire with them to award high marks to miracle because she was his girlfriend.

He also favours the girlfriends of his colleagues lecturers so that was a common and normal practice among them. miracle didn't make time to study. It's either a program to attend, going home to see her husband, or hanging out with her lecturers in their bungalows to warm their beds but when exam results are released, this lady scores higher grades in all courses taught by male lecturers and perform poorly in that of her female lecturers. This is one of the rots in our various tertiary institutions that must be looked at. No wonder the certificates are no longer recognized. A graduate will come out with good grades but cannot perform on the job. They need additional 'on the job' training before they could do something. The standards of our educational system has really fallen.

miracle was enjoying herself on campus whiles her husband was also boasting of a beautiful and rich wife in the University. Even the worst part of her relationship on campus was she being a mental patient without the lecturer knowing. miracle stopped taking her medications for sometime so symptoms of her Mania started popping up.

She could go to the general office of her department and ruin insults to the staffs if they did something against her interest. One day she met the head of the department and her actions of misconduct started. The head wanted to threaten her of dismissal if she didn't discipline herself. miracle insulted this man very well which must have called for her dismissal.

The exams officer came to her defense and advised that she must first be cross-examined by the counselling department. When that was done, they got to know that she was a mental patient. That was her luck. But the University deferred her course for a year which means she had to repeat that year when she returns.

At the time she was serving her suspension periods, she does travel with her husband to places. At times they were captured on TV on news segments and that alone makes her father feel self actualized. After a full year of marriage, she wasn't able to conceive. She told her husband that she wanted to graduate before getting pregnant so she was controlling herself.

Madam Faustina gave birth to a girl and we were invited to their naming ceremony. They were happy seeing us around. I told Mr Charles that I needed to give all the thanks to him because had it not to be him, I couldn't have married Gift.

miracle' husband was not happy about her wife's inability to get pregnant and this brought a quarrel between them. During one of their medical consultations, the assessment proved that she could give birth so probably, she needed some few time. When her husband's sperm was tested at the lab, the result indicated that his sperm was not strong enough to impregnate the lady.

It was good the man also tested himself for possible problems. Mostly when this happens, the men always blame the ladies for not being fertile. Pressure normally comes from the man's family on the woman to give birth. Some even suggest to the man to send the lady away whiles maybe the problem is from the man.

Junior Olorunsogo was also developing well. Because we both do not have enough time to stay at home, we sent him to a boarding school. Despite the fact that my performance in bed was not as it was before the accident, Gift managed me that way. She learnt a lesson from what she nearly got herself into with Mr Mike so she made her mind to accept me just the way I am. The only problem in bed was, I do get tired especially at the time she needed it the most. I went to the same forest to get the herb I made for Mr Charles.

Much improvement was felt but it still couldn’t be like it used to be.

One day at the boutique where I was attending to one customer, I noticed a lady entering the boutique. She looked familiar so I decided to go and verify if I knew her. Lo and behold, she was the lady I proposed to by the river side back in my village. She was the one I asked to meet at a drinking spot where she insulted me and made her friends to also laugh at me. “Lady can you recollect seeing me somewhere”, I asked. She looked at me from head to toe for a while and said not really.

“Are you not from Torve in the Volta region”?, I asked again. “Yes how come you know me? This is my first time of coming into this shop and you already know me.” She said surprisingly. “I’m Agbanavor the guy who asked you one morning by the river side and asked you to meet me at the drinking spot. Can you now remember?” “Yes yes yes, ei, you. So this is where you’ve been hiding. You have really changed, wow”, she said with joy.

I asked her what she needed and got them for her. I asked her to keep the money. She fell in love for me instantly. I equally felt some lust for her. I told her to be paying me visits whenever she is free. As time goes on, she does come to help me sell. I informed Gift about this but she was not happy about that.

One day she came to the shop during her break periods to see her sitting beside me. Looking at what my friend was wearing, Gift suspected something going on but I told her that there was nothing going on between us but Gift wouldn't believe me.

Chapter 7

Looking at what my friend was wearing, Gift suspected something going on but I told her that there was nothing going on between us but Gift wouldn't believe me. She picked quarrel with her at the shop. Without even asking further questions, she dropped her bag and faced Esther my childhood friend.

Gift: Look, sister, I won't sit down for you to break my home. Do you know where we started from? It will be better for you to send yourself out of this place before I descend on you.

Esther stood up from where she was sitting and positioned herself well with her hands on her waist.

Gift: Just look at what you are wearing, you are not even ashamed of yourself. How can you call this just a visit? You are the very people guys will infest deadly diseases with. You are lucky I'm in a good mood.

Esther: Madam I respect you enough that's why I just decide to keep quiet but if you want to force my other side out this afternoon, I will show you the profound one. How can you just come here and start insulting me? Who do you think you are? Who should even claim ownership of Agbanavor? You or I? Look, don't try me.

Gift: I will try you. If you are a lady like me open that your dirty mouth again and see who is who here.

Me: Sweetheart please it shouldn't get to that point. Esther, please leave.

Gift: Olorunsogo, but how could you? Have I not given you enough?

Me: Gift be careful with what you say. Have you caught me doing something with her? I won't take this disgrace from you again.

Gift: You call this disgrace right? Okay I've heard you. And you what are you still doing there?

Esther: Olorunsogo I will be waiting for you home. Pass by when you close I will give the best today.

Me: Hey! Esther don't come and give me any trouble. Have we agreed to anything like that? And where from that one too? Esther tell my wife what you just said is not true.

Gift: "Oyiwa"! I said it. Go and see her after that come to me in the house.

Gift took her bag and went to meet the bank's car driver for them to go. " Esther what have you just caused? How do you want me to explain this to my wife? " I asked.

“She thinks she can just insult me Esther, don't worry invite me to your house let me come and talk sense into her”. Without allowing her finish her sentence, I held her lips to stop talking. “Look that is my wife for Christ sake so don't just talk against her like that. I love her and wouldn't want to lose her. Don't come to this boutique again”, I cautioned her. She then left in shame.

I became very worried within myself because I don't know how I will be able to convince Gift that nothing of that sort was going on between Esther and I. The devil wouldn't let you to be free at any time so I will appeal to all believers not to stop praying because until the evil one gets you, it will never leave you. After work, I locked the boutique and went home. When Gift returned from work, she never said anything about what went on. She came to prepare food and ate hers at the kitchen.

She didn't serve me as she used to do. When I asked where my food was, she just looked into my face and went into the room to sleep. She didn't say a word and seriously speaking, I was getting more worried because how could I explain myself for her to understand? Hmm. I went into the kitchen, served myself and also ate at the kitchen. I watched Television for few minutes and went to join her in bed. I lied down facing the ceiling for solutions to this problem.

I was actually restless that night. I couldn't sleep. At dawn, I tapped her to wake up so that we talk. She said there was nothing to discuss and I was just coming to disturb her sleep. She didn't wake up to listen to what I had to say so I also decided to say what I had to say because I knew she could hear. I first started by apologizing for what happened the previous day. I went on to explain to her that what Esther said was just out of place. "Olorunsogo why are you disturbing my sleep? I'm not ready for any talk this morning", she said, took her cloth and went to sleep on the couch outside. From all indications, my apology was not accepted.

In the morning, she didn't prepare breakfast but left for work and without our usual goodbye kisses. This single life in marriage continued for almost a week. I decided to wait for her temper to calm down well before we talk about the issue. When I close from the boutique, I usually buy either fast food or fruits and that serves as supper. One morning, I wanted to toast some bread for breakfast before going to the boutique. In the process, I ended up burning the egg. She came to the kitchen and saw what I was doing. She smiled and just open the fridge to take her cornflakes.

As she turned to go, I quickly held her from behind. “Gift so for how long are we going to remain like this?” She turned to me and said, “until you notice the pain you’ve caused me. What don’t I do for you in this house? All you can do is to go sleeping with that slut. Let me go. I’m getting late for work.” I knelt before her and said “my dear, all what you are thinking of is not true.

Esther is just from my village. She came to buy clothes and just decided to visit. What she said the other time was just to tease you. So please forgive me and let’s come back to normal. I’m tired of this bachelor life”. “Look at how innocent you are looking. Please stand up. I’ve heard you but before everything can come to its normal state, you need to go for HIV test or anytime you want to have sex with me, you need to get your condoms ready”, she said. She prepared another toasted bread for me that morning before leaving for work.

A week later, Gift’s father called her and asked her to come home with immediate effect. I made up my mind to go with her. When we got there, we saw miracle in the house with a swollen face. When asked, her mother said her husband beat her because of her inability to give birth. “Oh no how come”?, I asked.

“Hey! My friend I didn’t invite you to be asking questions. By the way who even invited you here” Gift’s father asked. “In-law I’m sorry. I told Gift I will leave her behind but she shouldn't keep too long. miracle was beaten by her husband not because of her unproductivity but because he heard of the life she was living on Campus with her lecturers.

Chapter 8

Gift helped her to the hospital for treatment. At the hospital, Gift asked her what exactly happened. In tears like a baby crying for breast milk miracle narrated how it happened.

miracle: Sister, from day one that I got married to this man I never enjoyed him. Physically, he is the man any lady will want to be with but within him, hmm. He suffers premature ejaculation and also low sperm count. These things were revealed to him when we went for check up on why I was not getting pregnant.

The doctor prescribed some medicines for him which could make him prolong sex so that probably through that, he could accumulate more sperms to get me pregnant. Anytime he was home, I made sure I left school and satisfy him home. One day he came to pay me a visit on campus and there, I introduced him to my friends. Not knowing, some of my friends got jealous of me having such a rich man. They praised me for having such a guy. Before my husband left, I decided to wash down before seeing him off because I knew I wouldn't return early. In my absence, one of my friends took his contact and said she wanted to keep it in terms of any emergency. Few weeks after the visit, my friend started chatting with him on phone.

One day they planned meeting each other and at that their meeting, she told my husband that I've been sleeping around with my lecturers on campus and she was sure I once aborted a foetus for one of my lecturers. She insisted that was why I was not able to get pregnant. My friend tarnished my image and that got him very angry. Her purpose was to make my husband hate me so she could take my position. She did her best to take my husband from me. Fortunately for me, another friend of ours saw the two where they had the meeting which got her surprised. She came back and informed me of what she saw at the restaurant.

I couldn't believe it until my friend returned. When I confronted her, she said it was a mere coincidence they met. My husband was supposed to travel so what got me worried was why he was still around. I called his contact to confirm if he was around and it went through. The following morning, I went home to asked him what he was doing in a restaurant with my friend. He didn't seem cheerful when I got home and he questioned me about how many times I have aborted for my lecturers. His question went deep down into my spine because I wasn't ready for that. My daddy forced me for that act simply because of this marriage.

He started shouting at me when I decided to ignore him. His shouts irritated me so I told him the truth and the reaaon for my actions, as a way of defense. This was where he got furious at me and beat me mercilessly. Today is the third day of the incident. I tried to take care of myself indoors because I didn't want anyone to know I was beaten by my husband but my self-care was not enough so I decided to come home so mum could help me."

Gift: hmm miracle, so your rich husband did this to you. I'm sorry for you but he had no right to assault you like this. What is daddy saying about this because he forced you to marry him?

Miracle: He said if I were not to do anything bad to my husband, he wouldn't have beaten me. He only said he will arrange so that he will meet us and talk to the two of us in order to bring back peace into our house because he wouldn't want to receive that disgrace of his daughter gerring married not long ago and beaten by her husband.

Gift: He can't be serious. By the way I'm going to report him to the police because he can't just put the laws into his own hands and do whatever pleases him. For daddy I'm sure his adropause (male equivqlent of menopause) is eating into his senses. How could he see you in this condition and say if you did nothing wrong he wouldn't have beaten you? Are we not to scare the wolf before advising the goat? Let them discharge you first and I will carry the case from there.

miracle: alright sister. Thank you.

Before she was discharged, Gift asked the doctor to write an arrest warrant for her to send to the police so that they arrest miracle' husband. Back in their house, Gift made it clear that she was going to call on the police to deal with miracle' husband but their father was not in support of the idea. The reason was that, due to he marrying miracle, the number of contracts that miracle' husband recommends to him makes him more rich and superior in the community and beyond. I ignored all his claims and went ahead to report the case to the police. The police asked miracle and I to join them so they arrest him. miracle began to show some behaviour which made Gift angry.

miracle indicates they should leave the case because she couldn't stand seeing him been touched or fined by the police. When Gift called me to inform me of this, I only told her to respect her sister's view because issues of marriage must be handled on humanitarian grounds. Gift obeyed my view and dropped the case. She was very angry at her sister.

Interestingly, Gift decided to accompany her sister to her husband's place so that she could talk sense into the man. When they got there, this man was in the house with miracle' friend who informed him about miracle " life on campus. Within a week, they started going out. When miracle saw this, it was more than telling one that he/she missed heaven. She was shocked. Gift tried confronting the lady and all the man could say was that, no one can decide for him. If miracle could go about sleeping with other men, why shouldn't he also do same.

This is one thing we see in many marriages today. The couple try to play tit for tat with each other. miracle picked up another fight with her friend this time around and in fact the scene was not nice. Gift rebuked miracle' husband for the behavior he was demonstrating whilst miracle was also fighting with her friend.

Gift and the man's attention was not with them so the next thing they could see was that the fight between the two ladies was becoming severe to the extent that miracle' friend was able to bring miracle to the ground. The lady wore sunglasses so in the process of the fight, she ended up using the handle of the glass to stab miracle in-between her nose and eye.

miracle shouted for help which Gift rushed to her aid. Gift pushed the lady to the ground and started beating her. miracle' husband carried miracle into his car and drove her to the hospital. Gift just couldn't stand seeing how blood was gushing out of her sister. She joined them and went back to the same hospital they were coming from.

miracle was taken to the accident and emergency unit where she was admitted and some pints of blood was transfused to her. Gift quickly went to inform the doctor who gave out a police report for the arrest of the man. miracle was unconscious and didn't even know where she was. Gift called me to come over and seriously speaking, I wonder if miracle could see any longer.

Seeing her, I became very bitter with her husband and pushed for the man's arrest. Just as you know, this guy is very rich and everyone knows him so when he was arrested, he gave a very huge amount to the police in order to make it a foolish case. When the issue got to miracle' father, he now got to understand what he was looking for. I personally called him to come witness where her daughter was.

When he was taken into the ward to see his daughter in a bandage covering her face, he shed tears and said he will never forgive this boy for doing this to his daughter. "Where is he"? Gift asked him what he wanted to do but he ignored that question. "I said where is that bustard who had the guts to Touch my daughter? He did it the first time and I didn't take any action so he thinks he could do anything? I said where is he? Won't anyone tell me anything?"

Chapter 9

This man was moving up and down the corridor talking to himself. He vowed not to forgive his beloved son in-law. He went into his car and drove with top speed to his son in-laws house. He blew his car horn very loud when he got to the gate. When the gateman opened the gate, he nearly knocked him down, when entering.

Gift's father: Where is that idiot you call your boss? He angrily asked the gateman.

Gateman: "Master I respect you enough so don't make me to change. I've not even eaten yet. Why won't you tell me who you are before barking like a dog?"

Gift's father: How dare you refer to me as a dog? Oh so that idiot asked you to insult me when I come around. Oh okay I see. The two of you will rot in jail.

Gateman: Jail for what? I think you need to be sent to the psychiatric hospital for assessment because I'm sure all is not well in your head. My boss is not around can you please drive out?

Gift's father: I must not take you serious. Because I can see stupidity written all over you. I will go into that house and deal with him myself.

Gateman: Master if you want to make my work difficult for me I will not take it lightly with you. I will open the dogs at you.

Gift's father decided to go into the room to confront his son in-law this time around. Before he could step on the porch, the gateman opened one of their big dogs which rushed on Gift's father. I wish you were there to see how this old man was running. I'm sure he would've won a race if it was a competition. He run it into his car and rolled his glasses. All these while, miracle' husband was in the room packing to fly out of the country. He actually warned his gateman not to allow anyone into the compound but his gateman disobeyed and allowed this man in.

He came out to meet his father in-law. He ordered his gateman to send the dog back which he did. "Oldman why are you disturbing me in my compound? How can I help you"?, his son in-law asked. "Are you asking me how you could help me? Look, don't think because of your wealth you can just do anything at anytime. You will rot in jail if my daughter does not survive", Gift's father replied.

"Why didn't you tell me your daughter is just a whore? Look, you forced your daughter on me. Since I married her, I never felt any change within me to show I'm married. I can't continue to keep a lady that has aborted for men and continues to sleep with her lecturers. Please be going I will come to the hospital to see her. But, note one thing. I'm terminating all contracts I had with you because of this marriage. You told me your daughter was a virgin whilst you knew she had aborted. You even fueled it.

Secondly, I've realized your daughter has multiple boyfriends so let her go to them. I don't want her any more. Like father like daughter. "This was the biggest shock Gift's father had ever experienced. He couldn't talk because he knew he caused everything. When this gentleman was searching for a lady, Gift's father recommended miracle to him.

He went into some contracts with him and when his daughter behaves well in the marriage, Gift's father will become more wealthier than he was. "You will meet me in court." He said and drove away to the police station to report for the arrest of his son in-law. When the police saw the defendant's name, they knew if they should take up the case, they will get money because this guy will definitely shower them with more money.

He followed the police back to his son in-laws house only to meet his gateman alone. The police tortured the gateman when he was denying to give the police information about the whereabouts of his boss. He finally said the truth that his boss travelled out of the country the very moment the incident occurred. When Gift got to hear this, she gave directions as to how they could arrest the lady who caused everything. In her statement at the police station, Gift narrated how everything happened in the house.

The police went after miracle' friend in school and brought her to the station. When interrogated on how the whole thing happened, she made it clear that it was a payback to miracle because the lecturer miracle aborted for was also her boyfriend but miracle managed to snatch him away from her and due to that, she never gets good grades at school. She was asked to mention the lecturers name of which she did. The news became a topical issue on the University campus.

The lady was prepared to be taken to court for the law to give her the necessary punishment she deserved. Two weeks later, there was a court sitting and final verdict was given. She was given a ten year jail term with hard labour or a fine of Ghc 30,000.00 and serve five years in prison. Gift's husband was also placed on a wanted list. He was deported and arrested also.

miracle' husband had already gone ahead to give a huge sum of money to the judge who ruled the case. He only fined miracle' husband Ghc5,000.00 and that was all. The judge added that miracle husband take care of his wife. After two weeks, it became obvious that miracle could no longer see with her other eye. miracle blamed her father for all that was happening to her. She told the doctor who was attending to her that, her father forced her to get married to her husband.

The doctor invited miracle' father and rebuked that selfish behaviour in him. The doctor who was equally an elderly man explained to him that, he shouldn't have forced his daughter into such a marriage because of money.

He explained that the happiness of the two must be a paramount factor to consider. If the two do not love each other before going into the marriage, such things were bound to happen. The two can easily cheat on each other simply because there was no love. They are only together as friends with benefit.

miracle father regretted what he did and when he got home, he invited Gift and I to his house. He called a family meeting just as he used to do when I was staying with them but miracle was not part of that meeting because she was still on admission. He apologized for his behaviour towards me and Gift.

He said he wasn't conscious at the time he was doing all those things but what the doctor told him really touched his heart so he wanted to make peace with everyone. Interestingly, Junior raised his hands and said he had something to say. "Daddy, I did something that I was finding it difficult to tell anyone", he said. "My son talk to me what did you do"?, said his dad.

.

"I have a girlfriend in school. She called me yesterday in the evening and said she was pregnant for me. But my fear is that I only slept with her once without a condom but our other sections were with a condom so I'm not sure that pregnancy is mine." Junior said. Junior was in his second year in the high school. On campus, he used his father's worth to win the heart of many of his colleague ladies. He finally got one of them pregnant. "Junior so you are trying to tell me that you have impregnated someone's daughter at this stage. Oh! So you people have just planned to disgrace me.

Look I have had enough of you people. I've tried my best to put you at higher levels but you chose the other option. I have no hand in your issue. Since you love each other, try and marry her and look after her yourself. I'm not supporting you to do anything", his father ruled. I also raised my hands and said I had no problem with the family so I will continue to be the good husband I am to my wife and the good son in-law to the family. After the meeting, we went to the hospital to see miracle and fortunately, she was responding to treatment but with only one eye.

Three days later, I left like visiting my former boss because it had been long I saw him. When I got there, he was home with his wife and child. His father was very sick when I got there. He said they've been to almost all the hospitals both in Ghana and abroad but there was no improvement. He explained how the condition was and quickly I remembered a herb that could be used to treat it.

I went into the same forest to get the herbs and prepared the medicine for my boss' father. Few days later and to the glory of God, the old man recovered. Charles and his wife was more than happy. His father was also thankful to me. Due to this the old man said because he is old, he wanted me to be acting on his behalf with regards to his work. He gave me one of his cars again and registered my name as his partner in business. God is so good.

How will life be after many years of hustle for Olorunsogo? Will he be able to realize the vision of his late father? What will happen when he returns to his village?

Chapter 10

Honestly speaking, I least expected such honour. I thanked the family for the opportunity and also asked them to forgive me on what happened in the past. Madam Faustina said everything that happens is bent on a purpose. She said had it not to be the fact that, that incident happened, her husband wouldn't have given him the love and care he was showing to her at the moment.

She added that, the incident has also made her understood one or two issues of life. Charles himself was happy for me coming back into their family. He told his wife that I was the one who prepared the medicine for him before he could perform at night to expectation. He also thanked me for saving his father's life. I informed them about miracle' current health condition and they all sympathized with her.

I went home to inform my wife about the breakthrough which came our way. She was very happy for me. That night was more special. As a congratulatory gift, she took her time to make me satisfy her very well. I'm very sure Gift's second pregnancy was as a result. The following day, which was a Saturday, I went to see Mr Charles and his family with Gift, my wife. Our reason for the visit was to thank them again for accepting us once again; not for us to stay with them but for giving me that job offer.

After few minutes of chat, Mr Charles and his wife together with Gift, went to visit miracle at the hospital. The Charles family gave her some money to take of herself. I could see it that miracle was fully conscious despite she lost one of her eyes coupled with her mental condition. Gift was also happy she didn't lose her sister. Everyone around encouraged miracle that she will be fine. I sat beside her on the hospital bed and encouraged her that she shouldn't lose hope in life due to her current condition.

I told her that she was a lady every guy would have liked to go after, but due to her current condition, not all men will be ready to live with a lady without one eye functioning. I then made her understand that, in life, we need not to have too much love for money.

"It is very true you are coming from a very wealthy home but that does not guarantee you to marry someone who is equally as wealthy as your parents. Yes it is necessary you get someone who can take care of you but not necessarily equal to the worth of your parents. Not all the rich men you see out there are good men for marriage. Many of them experience difficulty remaining in one relationship and due to that, they cheat on their partners.

They squander money on these ladies simply because these same ladies are in for money. My advise to you now is, allow yourself for God to do His will in your life. If a man comes around and shows interest in you, your first judgement shouldn't be how rich he is, but rather check for how caring and loving that gentleman will be. We all know that it is the responsibility of every man to provide for the home. Once this man has the capability of providing for you and your children, I think that alone will be enough to start a relationship. You the lady can also help in building the home.

Even that will ensure some sort of security in the marriage because it will look like a partnership business. Another issue I will like to inform you about is the interference of friends in your marriage. Don't think *all* your friends wish you well in your marriage. Some of them feel jealous when you start to tell them more about the goodness in your husband.

You might not know what is going on in that friends relationship so because you project to her that your husband is the best, she can find ways and means to get herself closer to your husband and if God is not on your side, you will lose your husband to your friend just as it happened to you now.

Even if possible, cut off some of your friends which you can see that has the impetus of snatching men from wives. When you are fully okay and discharged from this place, think about all this I've told you today.

“miracle was shed tears as I was talking to her. She said she was sorry for everything that happened. She also regretted messing up her own life. “I am the cause of my problems. But my father also influenced me. The lecturer who got me pregnant would have married me but my father refused. Thank you for your advice”, she said. Mr Charles her former playboy also encouraged her.

After a week, I looked for someone to operate the boutique for us while I started work as a network marketing officer. From grass to grace. I never dreamt of wearing suit with tie in my life. And I never thought I could meet some top officials in this world. Due to my new work, I do travel to many places to advertise the company to people. My difficulty was on the English proficiency so I needed to upgrade myself. I do attend adult classes to learn how to read and write well at the age of 32.

Gift got pregnant and this time around, it was joy in the house. Junior Olorunsogo was also academically sound looking at his performance at school. I did advice him that he shouldn’t only memorize books and pass out from school. He should rather develop himself and be versatile. He should come out from school and be someone who can think and solve problems in society and not a graduate who only knows theories and has nothing to do when it comes to applications.

After establishing myself as a young man, I decided to visit my village, Torve. The problem was that apart from my unty's house, I had no other place to lodge because they've all disowned me. I waited for Gift to give birth to our second child who we named Ewornam. She happened to be a girl. Ewornam simply means my God has done it for me. Indeed God has done it for me. We turned good Christians as well and did attend church regularly. After Ewornam started walking, we travelled to my village.

The environment looked very different for me when I got there because it had been long I left there. I drove to my aunty's house and nothing has changed. Her old building remained the way it was but the unfortunate thing was that none of her children had gone very far in life. The best was living an average life and the ladies got married to some of the village folks and couldn't continue with their education.

When my aunty saw the car, she was surprised because she never expected in her life to see a private car coming into her compound. She stood and watched the car come into the house. When I packed, I asked Gift to go and ask about me from her. I said she should ask her my whereabouts so that we see her reaction. Gift got down and went to greet politely and asked where she could find me. "Oh it has even been long I remembered that name Olorunsogo. My dear, that boy happened to be my son but he left me to stay somewhere alone in the bush. One day we heard that he got missing from the village but I'm sure his father has come for him into eternity.

By the way why are you looking for someone who is no more"?, she surprisingly asked. As astonished as she was, Gift looked at her and came back into the car. I asked the children to come down and together with Gift we came down from the car. I walked and stood in front of my aunty and asked her if she could recognize me. She couldn't so I showed her a mark which was on my shoulder and asked her if she could recognize me. "Ah is this not Olorunsogo? Olorunsogo is this you"?,she asked. "Yes I'm Olorunsogo, aunt.

I'm not dead but I will continue to live to proclaim the goodness of God. This is my wife and children. We just want to visit you today. "My aunty bowed her head in shame and knelt before me.

"My son, please forgive me. I didn't know you were the one. We thought you were no more. I'm happy you've returned to your lovely aunty." She called my children and embraced them. She then gave us chairs to sit.

My brothers and sisters, they may plan or think evil for you but if God, who is the giver of life, does not give the go ahead, their plans will be in vain. My aunty thought I was dead so she even forgot about me. I made peace with her and asked about her children. She then narrated how things turned upside down for her when I left her. She said she no more get good harvest and also things became very difficult for her.

One thing about life is that, if you help someone to be a better person one day and if even the person did not reward you physically, God in heaven will reward you in so many ways. But if you don't want the progress of someone, don't expect yours to also be good. I heard the woman who first mentioned it that I was an evil child passed on some few years ago. I drove through the town and visited my old friends and my food vendors.

The first person to visit was the one who saw me leaving and asked of her money. I gave her a large sum of money for selling for me on credit during those days. Within two years I went to renovate my father's building and all projects he left behind. This was where people started introducing themselves to me as family members. Some will say they are my uncles, some brothers and sisters and a whole lot.

At the time I had no hope in life, none of these people showed up, but after my breakthrough, they started identifying themselves. I think it's high time we change our attitude towards the poor in society. We should help such people come out of that situation so that they can rather feel indebted to you than hide yourself when the person is struggling and if God bless the person, we come and say whole lots of things.

Money was there before we were born and will continue to be there after we die so in life, we shouldn't make ourselves slaves to it. Let's rather put our trust in God Almighty for the best. Four years of working for Charles' father, he passed on naturally. In his will, he mentioned my name in it.

He maintained my position for me in the business. He also added the car I was using to it so the car became mine and I was now working for myself. miracle got married to man of God who claimed he had been counseling her and got her pregnant again. The man of God was an average earner but they lived happily. miracle now became a woman of God and has been preaching to people especially the youth on how to take care of their lives so they don't go into what she went through in life.

The End.

www.ingramcontent.com/pod-product-compliance
Lightning Source LLC
LaVergne TN
LVHW050337160826
845677LV00014B/3647
9798353192053